# Mom and Me

Marla Stewart Konrad

WORLD VISION EARLY READERS

Tundra Books

Text and photographs copyright © 2009 by World Vision

*All royalties from the sale of this book go to support
World Vision's work with children.*

Published in Canada by Tundra Books,
75 Sherbourne Street, Toronto, Ontario M5A 2P9

Published in the United States by
Tundra Books of Northern New York,
P.O. Box 1030, Plattsburgh, New York 12901

Library of Congress Control Number: 2008903005

Library and Archives Canada Cataloguing in Publication

Stewart Konrad,
    Mom and me / Marla Stewart Konrad.
(World vision early reader series)
Target audience: For ages 2-5.
ISBN 978-0-88776-866-8

    1. Mother and child—Juvenile fiction. I. Title. II. Series.

PS8621.O55M64 2009      jC813'.6      C2008-902100-2

We acknowledge the financial support of the Government of
Canada through the Book Publishing Industry Development
Program (BPIDP) and that of the Government of Ontario through
the Ontario Media Development Corporation's Ontario Book
Initiative. We further acknowledge the support of the Canada
Council for the Arts and the Ontario Arts Council for our
publishing program.

ONTARIO ARTS COUNCIL
CONSEIL DES ARTS DE L'ONTARIO

Printed and bound in China

1 2 3 4 5 6      14 13 12 11 10 09

**Photo credits:**

**Cover:** Large – Jon Warren
          Small, from top to bottom – Violeta Roman, Rachel
          Wolff, Albert Yu, Kari Costanza, Laura Runcanu, Laura
          Runcanu, John Kisimir, Kari Costanza
**Title Page:** Kari Costanza
**Dedication Page:** Marco Cedillo

**Spreads**
I Love my Mom: Wah Eh Htoo, Mary Kate MacIsaac,
   Yahaira Masias
When she Goes Somewhere: Jon Warren, Jon Warren,
   Scott Lout
When I'm Hungry: John Kisimir, Philip Maher, Jon Warren
If I am Sad: Kate Scannell Michel, Kevin Cook, Jon Warren
When I Need a Wash: Raphael Palma, Jon Warren, Ryan Smith
When I Need Help: Andrew Goodwin, Andrew Goodwin,
   Jon Warren
She Let's Me Help: Jon Warren, Jon Warren, Sopheak Kong
Takes Me to School: Khuat Quang Hung, Jon Warren
She Helps Me: Andrew Goodwin, Jon Warren
We Share Smiles: Marco Cedillo, Andrew Goodwin,
   Pablo Carillo
Mom Loves Me: Sheryl Nadler

To my mom, Eileen Stewart-Rhude.

I love my mom. I know she is proud of me.

When she goes somewhere, she takes me along.

When I am hungry or thirsty, Mom is there . . .

. . . and if I am sad, Mom comforts me.

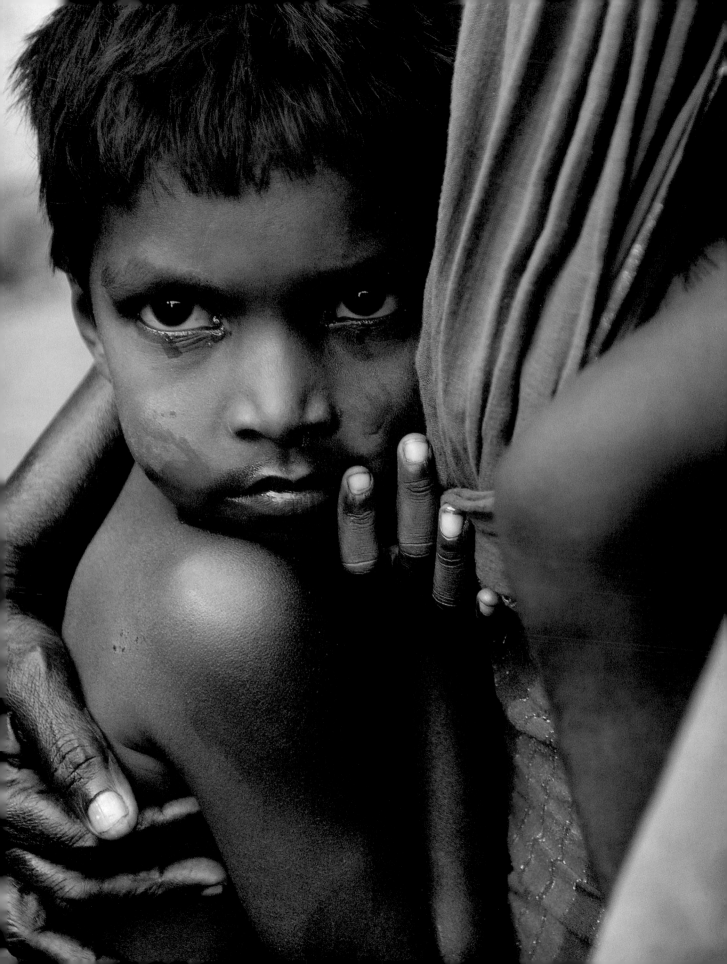

When I need a wash, she cleans me up.

When I need help, Mom shows me how.

Sometimes she even lets me help her!

Mom takes me to school.

She helps me with my homework.

We share smiles and kisses.

Mom loves me like no one else. Mom and me.